Original title:
Frosty Feud: Snowball vs. Ice Cube

Copyright © 2024 Creative Arts Management OÜ
All rights reserved.

Author: Simon Fairchild
ISBN HARDBACK: 978-9916-94-274-1
ISBN PAPERBACK: 978-9916-94-275-8

Winter's Wrath

In a snowy field, two pals collide,
One with a cube, the other with pride.
They hurl and they laugh, a chilly volley,
While neighbors look on, quite jolly and folly.

The cube rolls tight, oh what a sight,
But snowballs soar in a flurry of white.
With each toss and giggle, the battle ensues,
As frozen delights turn to icy shoes!

Frozen Frontlines

Amidst the drifts, a showdown so grand,
An icy launcher, a frosty hand.
Bob yells, "Watch out!" with a chuckle so bright,
While Jane lobs her snow with all of her might.

They scurry and tumble, the snow flying high,
A slippery dance under the gray winter sky.
No one's the victor, just laughter and fun,
In this whimsical duel, they all weigh a ton!

Sleighbell Skirmishes

On a sled ride down, with grins on their faces,
Two frosty warriors claim icy bases.
They load up their ammo, with giggles galore,
As snowballs fly fast, causing chaos and more.

With each little splash, they erupt into glee,
The crisp winter air is as joyful as can be.
Oh what a ruckus, snowflakes in flight,
In this playful rattle, the world feels just right!

Chill Winds of Change

As the wind whistles through, the battle ignites,
Snowballs are soaring, oh what funny sights!
The ice cube rolls on, trying to keep speed,
While snowflakes dance like they're plotting a deed.

With each little tumble, a giggle erupts,
These frosty shenanigans can't be corrupt.
Laughter rings loud, a glorious sound,
As friends make memories in snow all around!

Frigid Feuds

In a world of snowflakes, two foes arise,
One's round and fluffy, the other, a surprise.
With laughter and giggles, they prepare to throw,
A ball full of mischief, watch it fly and glow.

But Ice Cube's not worried, he's sturdy and slick,
His icy demeanor, he'll flaunt like a trick.
Snowball comes bounding with zest and with glee,
"Catch me if you can, oh icy decree!"

The Icy Impasse

In the playground of winter, it's a riot, you see,
Where snow and ice clash, oh what a spree!
One rolls and one slides, in the frigid air,
Who will reign victor? It's anyone's dare!

With a splash of cold laughter, the duel's underway,
They're tossing and turning in a playful ballet.
Snowball takes aim, with a flick of the wrist,
While Ice Cube just jests, saying, "I'll persist!"

Frosty Face-off

In the land of the chilly, where giggles abound,
A battle of snow and ice, laughter is found.
The sun peeks shyly, just warming the scene,
While the two frosty champs get ready to be seen.

Snowball's so playful, he bounces with cheer,
Ice Cube stands firm, with a grin ear to ear.
"I'm solid and steady, watch me take a stand!"
"I'm swift and I'm jolly, just try if you can!"

Shards of Chill

With giggles and snowflakes, they dart to and fro,
Two frosty competitors, putting on a show.
With snowballs a-flying and ice cubes in tow,
Who will be the champion? Only time will show.

In this shards of chill, they spark a bright fight,
Amidst all the chuckles that blanket the night.
Each toss a delight, a laughter-filled chase,
Let's cheer for our heroes in this frosty place!

Frozen Duel

In a winter land so bright,
Two foes prepare for a fight.
One's a ball of fluff and cheer,
The other's slippery, oh dear!

They launch their arms with icy glee,
Laughter ringing, just wait and see.
The snowball flies, the cube slips by,
Each one aiming to make the other cry.

Who's the victor in this game?
It's all in good fun, not for fame.
With frosty laughs and chilly grins,
The battle ends, let the fun begin!

Battle of the Blizzards

A blizzard roars, the stage is set,
For a clash that we won't forget.
Fluffy projectiles fill the air,
While icy cubes just glide with flair.

Who could throw the best, we shout,
As snowy clouds begin to sprout.
The coldest chuckles fuel the fight,
While wintry warriors take their flight.

Frosty flakes get stuck in hair,
As laughter echoes everywhere.
The battle rages, spirits high,
With friendly foes who wave goodbye.

Ice Showdown

Gather round, the chilly rings,
Where winter's jesters pull their strings.
A snowball rolls with glee and grace,
An ice cube bounces, quickens pace.

They leap and dodge in playful dart,
In this duel, they're off the chart!
With frosty throws and slippery spins,
Who will claim the win? Let's begin!

Cheers for the snow, applause for the ice,
With every landing, the laughter is nice.
Though cold as the North, the joy is warm,
In this showdown, there's no alarm!

Snowy Showdown

In a park where snowflakes drift,
Two champions prepare for the gift.
One's fluffy, round and light as air,
The other's slick, like a frosty stare.

They charge with glee, both on their toes,
Making quick picks of their snowy foes.
A cube collides with a smushy blast,
While giggles and thrill, build up fast.

Around the trees, their laughter races,
Battling through snowy spaces.
Who will stand tall when it's done?
In this chilly rumble, it's all in fun!

Frozen Rivalry in Winter's Embrace

In the park where laughter reigns,
Two frosty foes take the reins.
One round and cheerful, soft as cream,
The other sharp, a frozen dream.

With giggles loud and cheeks aglow,
They toss and whirl, the fun will grow.
A whack! A splash! The crowd does cheer,
As winter's whim takes center here.

The round one giggles, bounces back,
While the block stands firm, not off track.
Who will win the playful bout?
In snow and ice, there is no doubt.

When the day ends with rosy cheer,
They share a laugh, no hint of fear.
For winter games, both bring delight,
In this chilly dance of purest light.

The Battle of Chilling Forms

In the midst of winter's charm,
Two chilly forms come to harm.
One rolls and tumbles with delight,
The other stands tall, ready to fight.

With silly names and frosty grins,
Each round begins, let the fun spin!
They launch their attacks with a quirky flair,
While laughter rings through the crisp air.

Round one circles, full of glee,
While square one plots and waits to see.
With every throw and every toss,
Who's the victor? Who's the boss?

But as the sun begins to fade,
They laugh and play, no need for shade.
For in this game, the joy remains,
Even when winter's cold refrains.

Flurry of Flavors in the Cold

Under skies of sparkling white,
Two types of frost find pure delight.
One wears the coat of swirling snow,
The other's icy, but stealing the show.

They toss and spin, create a mess,
In a world of winter's soft caress.
The round one rolls, oh what a view,
While the cube stands strong, like it's all true.

They scream and shout, it's time to play,
As snowflakes dance through the day.
With silly faces, cheeks aglow,
This winter battle steals the show.

And when the last round hits the ground,
Their laughter echoes all around.
In this frosty game, so bold and bright,
Friendship wins, as day turns to night.

Arctic Altercations: Sphere vs. Block

In a land where snow gleams white,
Two frosty foes bring pure delight.
One's a sphere with wiggle and sway,
While the block stands strong, ready to play.

With frosty giggles and scattered snow,
These chilly rivals steal the show.
They dance around in gleeful cheer,
Creating memories, year after year.

With every toss and playful jab,
They pop and crack, oh what a gab!
The round one rolls, the square one stacks,
Each little hit brings laughter back.

Yet when the sun begins to set,
They share a laugh, no hint of regret.
For in their hearts, they know it's true,
Winter's magic brings friends anew.

Glimmers of Grit

In the park where winter plays,
Snowballs launch in snowy haze.
With giggles bright and laughter loud,
Two kids stand strong, both feeling proud.

Round and round the icy fight,
Ice cubes roll with all their might.
They slip and slide, what a scene,
A frosty clash, oh so keen!

With every toss, a flurry flies,
Little giggles, silly cries.
A snowman topples with a thud,
The ground is pure, a snowy mud!

In the end, they shake and grin,
Friendship rules, let the games begin!
With frosty breath and frozen toes,
They laugh aloud, that's how it goes!

Windswept Rivalry

Up on hills where breezes blow,
Snowball fights begin to grow.
With squinted eyes, they take their aim,
Each icy missile a new claim to fame.

But watch out for the icy crew,
Rolling cubes, a sneaky few.
They dance around like little spies,
Ready to surprise with quick, cold pies!

Tumbling laughter fills the air,
As snowmates race without a care.
They slip and slide on frosty ground,
In laughter's grip, they're glory-bound!

When the battle calls an end,
They hug and shout, let's be friends!
In the chill, their hearts ignite,
In snowy lands, they find delight.

The Shiver Show

Gather 'round for a chilly show,
Snowballs fly, best friend or foe?
With icy giggles and snowflakes bright,
Watch the spectacle take flight!

And here come cubes, all stacked so high,
Rolling slick, oh my, oh my!
Deciding who will take the crown,
With winter's breath, they throw it down!

A puff of snow, a slushy splash,
Someone's grandma joins the clash!
Taking aim with such a grace,
Cold and laughter, what a place!

When the last round ends in cheer,
Chilly smiles from ear to ear.
With memories made of frosty glow,
Life's a laugh in the shiver show!

Cold Hearts Collide

Amidst the flakes, a dance unfolds,
With frozen fingers, brave and bold.
Snowballs whirl, a sparkling flight,
Battles fought till the fall of night.

Ice cubes shiver, what a sight,
Rolling in with pure delight!
They're slippery creatures on the go,
Creating chaos in the snow!

With laughter ringing in the air,
Silly faces, no time to care.
Each frosty toss, a prankish move,
As kids around twirl and groove!

When all is done, they laugh and share,
Their frozen hearts, a joyful pair.
In the winter's chill, they smile wide,
Friendship blooms where cold hearts collide!

Whispering Frost: The Duel of Elements

In the winter's playful chill,
A round sphere with a frosty thrill.
It rolled with glee, a snowy charm,
While icy cubes planned to disarm.

With laughter echoing through the air,
The round one danced without a care.
The square sat tight, plotting a fall,
In this chuckling, chilly brawl.

As flakes of white began to swirl,
The round one twirled, a snowy whirl.
The squares just stood, all stiff and neat,
Preparing for a frosty feat.

But soon the round one zipped and zoomed,
While cubes just sat, feeling doomed.
In this duel of chill and cheer,
The snowball laughed—victory near!

Cold Conflict: Round vs. Square

On a playground of white, a showdown is set,
A ball of snow with no hint of regret.
Against a cube, so stiff and square,
Who will emerge in this frosty air?

The snowball rolls with playful delight,
Darting and dodging, oh what a sight!
While cubes just clank with a stubborn frown,
Wondering how to take the crown.

The snowball launches, a joke on the breeze,
With giggles and gales that aim to please.
The icy squares try to hold their ground,
But slippery laughter is all around.

In the end, a splash and a splat,
The squared ones melted—imagine that!
While round and jolly, the victor's cheer,
Echoed through winter, loud and clear!

Glacial Grudge Match

In a frosty arena, two foes prepare,
One round and playful, the other quite square.
With winter's energy crackling alive,
It's a comical clash, a frosty strive.

The ball of snow, a cheeky sprite,
Flung high in the air, what a glorious flight!
The square just grumps, plotting its scheme,
But laughter erupts—it's all just a dream!

A snowball whizzes, a missile of fun,
While cubes just quiver, no joy on the run.
As winter wind howls, the round one displays,
Winning the crowd with its frosty ballet.

And when the fun settles, snow gently gleams,
The icy cubes melt, losing their dreams.
With giggles retreating, they can't help but cheer,
For in this grand match, the spirits are clear!

The Snowball's Flight Against the Ice

A snowy delight rolls into the fray,
Daring the squares to join in the play.
With a chuckle and roar through the crisp afternoon,
The snowball smiled, eclipsing the moon.

The cubes stood stoic, no wiggle or sway,
Watching the round one, so eager to play.
Then with a flick, the snowball took wing,
While squares just wobbled, not quite in the swing.

The icy contestants would soon come undone,
As silliness reigns in the winter sun.
With each frosty toss and each wheezy laugh,
The snowball just danced, writing its path.

At last, when the sun lit the melting ground,
The snowball winked as the cubes flopped down.
In a blizzard of giggles, round takes the day,
In this comical clash where frost won the play!

Frigid Fray

In winter's chill, they take their stand,
A ball of snow in each hand.
With laughter loud, they start the chase,
While icy shards bring smiles to face.

The snowballs fly, a flurry bright,
Bounce and tumble, what a sight!
But ice cubes spin with frosty grace,
Slipping 'round in a slippery race.

With each cold throw, giggles erupt,
As frozen foes are hopelessly stuck.
Laughter rings through the breezy air,
Who'll win this frosty affair?

The snow settles thick, their battle done,
What a riot, oh what fun!
With frozen hands and cheeks aglow,
They vow to play on in the snow.

Crystal Combat

A snowy landscape, pure and white,
Two frosty teams prepare to fight.
With laughter echoing through the trees,
They launch their bombs, "Take that!" with ease.

Ice cubes scatter in disarray,
While snowballs fly and twist and sway.
The laughter rings, a joyful sound,
As snowy enemies spin around.

With every toss, a splat and squish,
They form a heap, oh what a wish!
To save the day, with snow and ice,
Each battle costs a bit of spice.

The duel is wild, yet filled with cheer,
The playful fight draws everyone near.
In winter's grip, with grins so wide,
They've built a joyful bumpy slide.

The Slippery Skirmish

The scene is set in white delight,
For slippery battles, a frosty fight.
With snowflakes swirling in the air,
Their frosty weapons drawn with care.

A snowball flings, it's quick and neat,
While icy cubes lend added heat.
They chase each other, round and round,
With laughter filling up the ground.

Who's on top? Who's hit the most?
In this chilly showdown, they love to boast.
A tumble here, a slip, a slide,
With rosy cheeks, they take it in stride.

At last, the fight begins to fade,
As sunlit skies begin to invade.
They hug it out, no foe to see,
Just friends in winter, wild and free.

Flurries of Fury

In a land of chill, two teams converge,
Where snowball flurries start to surge.
With grimy gloves and glee abound,
Winter's battle soon is found.

The ice cubes clash with splashes bright,
As snowballs zoom, their targets in sight.
The giggles echo, a playful bell,
In this frosty kingdom, all is well.

They spin and roll, each one a jest,
The snow-mound warriors giving their best.
With icy missiles soaring high,
They laugh aloud beneath the sky.

When fun concludes and day turns dim,
They shake hands and share a whim.
For every throw in winter's haze,
Makes memories that forever blaze.

Arctic Altercation

Two frosty foes in a glimmering field,
One packs a punch, the other won't yield.
With a whoosh and a toss, the laughter ignites,
As snowballs take flight on those wintry nights.

A slippery slide, oh what a sight,
One cube goes rolling, but oh, what a fright!
They tumble and giggle, dancing in glee,
While the winds howl a tune, wild and free.

But silence falls short as the squabble begins,
With icy remarks and mischievous grins.
From fortress to fortress, the battle's denied,
In the warmth of their laughter, no need to decide.

As the sun peeks out, the truce gets declared,
With high-fives of snow, no one is spared.
The chill of the air can't freeze their delight,
In a winter wonderland, they play through the night.

Ice Shaker

In a dance of delight, two rivals appear,
One's fluffy and round, the other's quite sheer.
They shake and they rattle, with giggles that burst,
Who will emerge, quenched of all thirst?

The ball flies in arcs, as the cube starts to roll,
With a whump and a splat, they both take a poll.
Who's winning the game? They can't quite agree,
Yet they both burst with joy, oh such revelry!

Each flake is a witness to mischief shared wide,
As the laughter erupts, the chill's pushed aside.
With icicles dangling, a chorus of cheer,
In a whirlwind of fun, nothing's to fear!

The curtain will drop on this frosty affair,
But their hearts are forever in winter's great lair.
So throw your hands up, and join in the throng,
For the ice and the snow bring a melody strong!

Chilly Exchange

Children of winter, the bravest array,
With snowballs and cubes coming out to play.
"Can you catch me?" one shouts, as they leap with a grin,

While the other just chuckles, "Watch where you spin!"

They clash with a pop, their frost-laden cheer,
As giggles erupt, making snowmen appear.
With a flick and a fling, they wrestle the white,
In this whimsical clash, oh what a delight!

Tumbling and slipping, the ground is a dance,
The cube wobbles 'round, in some sort of trance.
It's a chilly exchange, with laughter galore,
"Wait, that was my cube!" "Well, now it's a score!"

As the sun starts to dip, the fun winds to close,
With memories carved in the snow that they chose.
No need for a victor in this frozen bazaar,
For joy's the true treasure, and they made it so far!

The Icebound Battle

In winter's grip, the chill is real,
Two foes emerge, ready to squeal.
One's a ball, round and white,
The other's sharp, a chilling sight.

They hurl with glee, oh what a sight,
Laughter echoes through the night.
Who will prevail, who will fall?
Snow whirls up, a frosty brawl.

The ground is slick, the stakes are high,
An icy victory, oh my, oh my!
A slippery slide, a tumble, a roll,
Cheering crowds, they lose control.

With every throw, the fun's unleashed,
A winter game, a frosty feast.
In this arena, joy holds sway,
As snow and ice have their play.

Sleet Slick Standoff

Under the clouds, the mischief brews,
Snowballs aim like clever cues.
Ice cubes clink, they plot their scheme,
While frozen forts become the dream.

With a flurry of fluff, they dash and dive,
Splat! A snowball's the perfect surprise.
The cubes retaliate, a slippery glide,
As laughter erupts, they cannot hide.

The frosty air, it crackles bright,
Chasing each other with pure delight.
Who knew that frost could spark such cheer?
In this rivalry, the fun's sincere.

A flake of kindness shines through the haze,
Even foes find their playful phase.
With every throw, they trade the glee,
In this winter, they're wild and free.

The Cold Arena

In the frozen court, the games begin,
A snowy giggle hides each grin.
With fluffy ammo stacked up high,
The ice grows quiet, the shouts imply.

With a launch and a toss, the crowd goes wild,
Each icy weapon, a winter's child.
As they deliver, a cheer erupts,
In this ruckus, the tension disrupts.

One foe's slippery, the other a bard,
With laughter in bombs, this isn't too hard.
The arena glows under starry pride,
While snowmen cheer from the frosty side.

They dance through chaos, the ultimate jest,
With ice-cold splashes, they're feeling blessed.
In playful skirmish, they cover the ground,
Life's a snowy ball, where joy is found.

Shimmering Rivalries

In a world of frost, the rivals play,
Shimmering mischief on display.
A snowball whizzes with friendly grace,
Ice cubes follow, each in their place.

With each toss, the wintry air sings,
Snowflakes dance, while laughter clings.
They duck and weave, a zany race,
In this laughable cold embrace.

With every round, they cheer and shout,
For what is fun without a bout?
The winter chill can't freeze the cheer,
As frozen friends hold laughter dear.

So on they go, with frosty flair,
In their icy kingdom, without a care.
The shimmering fun that winter brings,
Ignites the joy in all their flings.

Wintry Warfare

In the yard, they gather their troops,
Snowballs stacked high like playful goops.
Laughter rings out as they take aim,
Ice cubes wait, their endgame a game.

A frozen barrage, the battle begins,
Squeals of delight as each one spins.
The air filled with giggles and zest,
Who will concede? Let's put them to test!

With slushy surprises and sneak attacks,
Dodging the plops as they launch back.
Chaos reigns in this chilly spree,
Victory dance, but who will it be?

At day's end, they collapse in a heap,
Snow-covered warriors, oh what a leap!
Lively memories in the soft, white glow,
Battle of laughter in the frosty flow.

Powdered Rivalry

Here they come, a wild crew,
Armed with snow, ready to pursue.
Lumps of white flying through the air,
Ice cubes plotting, a crafty affair.

One tosses high and the other ducks,
Bouncing off walls like playful luck.
Crunchy chaos, a flurry of fun,
With each snowball, another home run.

The gleeful shouts rise up to the sky,
Frosty foes laugh, oh how they fly!
As ice cubes sparkle, plotting their strike,
Who would have thought it'd be such a hike?

In a slip and slide, they tumble down,
Covered in flakes, no hint of a frown.
The ultimate showdown, a whimsical tale,
As friends come together, they'll prevail.

Glacial Grudge

A mountain of snow, a fortress of might,
Cubes conspire, plotting their flight.
With giant snowballs rolling nearby,
They launch their attack with a gleeful cry.

Little fingers grasp in a snow-filled fight,
A sprinkle of powdered delight!
One side laughing, the other in jest,
Who will emerge as the very best?

Splats and giggles fill up the day,
A wintery brawl in the frosty play.
As snowflakes twirl in the cool, crisp air,
Rivalry serves to lighten the glare.

When the sun sets on this merry clash,
They shake hands with a friendly bash.
With cheeks rosy and joy in each heart,
This snowy rivalry, a true work of art!

Snowball Saga

Once upon a time in the snow,
Two tiny armies ready to throw.
Snowballs primed for the silliest fight,
While ice cubes gleam with mischievous light.

Puffs of powder fly all around,
They're ducks and they're dodging on soft, frozen ground.

The hilarity builds with each comical fling,
Who will taste victory? Let's hear the bell ring!

They giggle and stumble, no fear in their eyes,
As snowballs soar like joyous surprise.
With icy opponents, they strategize bold,
In this whimsical war, a story unfolds.

At twilight's arrival, they shake off the frost,
In a world made of laughter, no one's the lost.
Through frosty fun, their spirits unite,
In a tale of pure joy under stars shining bright.

Subzero Struggles

In a world of white, they fight with glee,
Snowball flies high, as wild as can be.
Ice Cube laughs hard, with a chilling grin,
Bring it on, buddy, let the fun begin!

Chasing each other through drifts of cold,
Laughter erupts, as the story unfolds.
Slippery slips, oh what a sight,
Bounce back up, ready to ignite!

With every toss, the stakes get higher,
Snowball's aiming, his heart's on fire.
Ice Cube deflects with a sparkly shield,
In this frosty clash, neither will yield!

As night falls down, they lay side by side,
Shivering giggles, no need to hide.
Under the stars, they recount the bliss,
In the chill of night, it's a frosty kiss!

Battle of the Blades

Two figures gleam, with edges so sharp,
Skating and sliding, they'll make their mark.
One is a ball made of fluffy delight,
The other a cube, all crisp and tight.

They swirl in circles, their moves are grand,
With frosty footwork, they take a stand.
Ice Cube skates fast, he's slick and quick,
While Snowball spins, pulling off a trick!

A clash of cool, they dance through the snow,
With muffled giggles, they put on a show.
Each step and spin, draws cheers from the crowd,
As the winter winds blow, they laugh out loud!

At the end of the day, both weary and worn,
They rest on the ice, together reborn.
Though one may roll, and the other's a slide,
In this frosty battle, they're both filled with pride!

The Winter's Edge

On the frosty edge, two rivals stand,
One's fluffy and fierce, the other's so bland.
Snowball bounces, with seeds of fun,
Ice Cube glistens, ready to run.

With a whistle and shout, the showdown's begun,
Snowflakes swirl down, dancing, oh what fun!
Each icy blast sends shivers around,
As laughter erupts, in this snowy playground.

Snowball takes aim, a perfect arc,
Ice Cube ducks low, avoiding the mark.
They leap and they spin, in the cold of the night,
Chasing each other 'til the morning light.

Together they play, no victors in sight,
Under the moon, it's a magical night.
With giggles and grace, they conquer the chill,
In this wintery realm, there's warmth in the thrill!

Snowstorm Spar

Amidst the snow, two champs engage,
Laughter and chaos take center stage.
Snowball thunders with frosty cheer,
Ice Cube replies with a chuckle sincere.

They twirl and tumble, a fabulous clash,
With puffs and shouts, their rivals will splash.
One's fluffy brilliance, one's icy cool,
In this wintery brawl, they break every rule!

From snow drifts high, to icy peaks,
The battle rages as laughter speaks.
They're dashing and crashing, a wild delight,
Chased by winter's whispers through the night.

As dawn breaks bright, and the spar winds down,
Both champions grin, wearing victory's crown.
In this frosty dance, they find their way,
For it's not about winning, but joy in the play!

The Great Ice Divide: Cubes and Balls

In a winter wonderland, kids took their stance,
Cubes of ice ready, they fancied a chance.
Snowballs went flying, with laughter and cheer,
One hit a cube, now it vanished, oh dear!

Cubes plotted attacks, perfectly square,
While balls rolled around like they just didn't care.
A clash in the park, oh what a delight,
Who will win, in this frosty freeze fight?

Snowmen watched closely, with carrot-nosed glee,
As ice-skated figures danced wild and free.
A slippery battle, with giggles and shouts,
In the heart of the winter, there were no doubts.

The sun peeked out, as the fun escalates,
In the sparkling white, fun competes with fates.
Who knew ice cubes could be so much fun?
With snowballs in tow, the chaos's begun!

Chill Wars: The Shape of Cold

Tiny warriors clash on the icy terrain,
Cubes roll their edges, but balls leave a stain.
A snowman referee yells, 'Let the games start!',
With each icy volley, they're playing it smart.

Snowball gigs got a round of applause,
Cubes aimed to catch, but, oh, what a pause!
Slippery patches thrown into the mix,
Splats of cool laughter that nobody kicks!

The frostbitten air was filled with their yells,
Round after round, like glorious elves.
As snow froze their toes, they kept up the chase,
They built mighty forts, in this chilly embrace.

With every bright toss, new sides took a stand,
In the riotous fun, they all made a band.
Snowball or cube, it's all good to play,
Win or lose, it's a glorious day!

Battles Beneath the Snowy Veil

Under a thick blanket of shimmering frost,
The battle raged on, with no one the boss.
Cubes stacked on towers, like ice-cube giants,
Snowballs amassed ranks, with cheeky defiance.

A slippery slope became the grand stage,
Where powder and slush met in a frosty rage.
They ducked and they dived, with snowflakes for shields,

In this madcap melee, no one could yield.

Suddenly a snowball flew with great speed,
Smacking a cube, what a reckless deed!
Laughter erupted, as snowflakes did hug,
The moments of joy turned the conflict to snug.

With twinkles above, they danced on the ground,
In a merry old tussle, with fun all around.
No grudges held here, just pure snowy cheer,
In the heart of winter, the best time of year!

Frostfire: The Rivalry Under Ice

In the heart of winter, a chill in the air,
Cubes and snowballs found themselves in a glare.
With frosty determination, they gathered their ranks,
To stage a grand battle, to give thanks to pranks.

Cubes stood all rigid, with edges so neat,
While snowballs rolled over, all fluffy and sweet.
They flung and they laughed in this whimsical throng,
Making frosty mayhem, where all could belong.

In the grip of the cold, there bloomed a new bond,
With sprinkles of snow, responses so fond.
Each miss or direct hit, fueled playful delight,
As laughter erupted all throughout the night.

So the icy skirmish turned light as a feather,
In the glorious chaos, they rallied together.
For whether you're cube, or a ball made of snow,
Under this frosty sun, the friendship will glow!

The Winter Brawl

A snowball flies with a gleeful shout,
But ice cubes clink, ready for a rout.
Laughter echoes in the chilly air,
As frosty warriors wage their playful dare.

Fluffy white missiles soar with great glee,
While frozen foes plot with a sly decree.
A tumble here, a slippery slide,
In this wacky battle, all take pride.

Chill laughter rings as snowballs stack,
While ice cubes counter with a frozen whack.
Who will win this jovial chase?
It's hard to tell in this frosty race!

The showdown ends with a heartfelt grin,
For in this brawl, no one really wins.
Just joyful chaos in winter's embrace,
A grand spectacle that time can't erase.

Snowdrift Dispute

Two sides gather on a snowy hill,
One with cheer and one with chill.
Snowballs gather, soft and round,
While icy cubes march with a thunderous sound.

They launch their rounds with a giggle and cheer,
Laughs ring out as they draw near.
Round and round, the battle swings,
In this frosty clash of comical things.

Snowflakes dance as tensions rise,
With frozen chuckles and playful lies.
Who slipped on ice or got hit with frost?
In this merry brawl, we laugh at the cost!

Finally weary, they call it a night,
Together they laugh in soft moonlight.
For here in the snow, on this chilly scene,
Friendship blooms where they once were mean.

Crystalized Conflict

Gather 'round, as the skies turn gray,
Snowballs and ice cubes come out to play.
With frozen grins and coats so thick,
This hilarious rivalry's bound to stick.

A snowball rolls, gaining great speed,
While ice cubes shuffle, plotting their deed.
Chortles burst forth with each silly blunder,
As snowflakes join in, twirling like thunder.

With goofy throws and playful lobs,
They scatter and slip, oh how the fun robs!
Icicles cringe as laughter ignites,
In this winter wonder, pure joy ignites.

In the end, they share a warm drink,
Forgotten jests, no time for a stink.
For winter's battle is best with a pal,
Where laughter is king, and we all have a gal.

Glacial Grit

Two frosty teams with a glint in their eye,
Snowballs ready, ice cubes standing by.
Chilly breezes carry the sounds of delight,
As snow and ice clash in this wintery fight.

Fluffy orbs fly and gracefully spiral,
While cubes skitter around, so viral.
Giggles erupt with each icy smash,
Whirling shouts as the snowflakes clash.

The humor thickens like a frosty glaze,
In the snowy arena, everyone plays.
Who will win? Oh, it's hard to tell,
As laughter and friendship ring the loud bell.

As night falls softly, they gather with care,
Swapping snow tales in the cool, crisp air.
For in these battles, it's friendship, you see,
That turns icy rivals to old pals, carefree.

Chill-Challenged

Two foes met on a snowy plain,
One was round, the other plain.
With laughter echoing through the air,
They launched their icy wares with flair.

A snowball dashed, a quick surprise,
While the cube just sat, no need for lies.
Then with a slip, oh what a sight,
The cube rolled down, quite the delight!

Frosty giggles danced around,
As they slung their icy rounds.
In this playful, snowy game,
Laughs and cheers were quite the fame.

With each throw, a winter's cheer,
No real worries, only good cheer.
Just two friends, enjoying the cold,
In their frozen land, so bold!

The Arctic Tussle

In a land where snowflakes swirl and glide,
Two icy challengers took to the slide.
One with curves, so fluffy and bright,
The other, sharp, ready for a fight.

With giggles and grunts, they took their stance,
A chilly brawl, a wintry dance.
The round one flew through the crisp, clear air,
While the cube just bounced, with little care.

Landing with splat, oh how they rolled,
Each flurry of fun turning ice to gold.
With frosty comebacks, they dodged and leaped,
Creating a storm, laughter never ceased.

In the end, no victor to claim,
Just two friends caught up in the game.
Snowflakes jumped in a joyful parade,
As they laughed in bliss, their battles displayed!

Hailstorm Havoc

When the skies turned grey and snowflakes poured,
Two frozen foes eagerly explored.
One a ball, full of giggles and cheer,
The other a cube, no corner to fear.

With icy shapes flying left and right,
Their playful war became quite a sight.
Each hit met with squeals of delight,
As they tumbled and twirled in the drifting white.

From behind the trees, they plotted their throws,
Quick as a flash, where nobody goes.
A momentary truce, a snowman was formed,
With a carrot nose, in laughter they warmed.

But soon they resumed their frosty duel,
In a flurry of fun, like kids back in school.
No winners here, just joyous spree,
In this stormy world, happy as can be!

Frostbite Fracas

With a chilling breeze, the stage was set,
Two icy rivals, no hint of regret.
One packed with power, the other with grace,
In this snowy arena, a silly race.

Dodging each other, they laughed and spun,
With each little fling, oh, so much fun!
A spectacle of splats and giggles galore,
As their snowy shenanigans stirred up a score.

Fumbling with snowballs, they took aim and shot,
But a cube's flat edge? It hit the right spot!
As they bickered and bantered with feigned despair,
Their laughter rang out, filling the frosty air.

With cheeks all aglow and breaths full of mist,
No reason to argue, no way to resist.
Just playful friends, taking on the freeze,
In their winter kingdom, where laughter's the key!

Icebound Ironies

In winter's grip, they took their stance,
A snowy orb doing a little dance.
An icy block rolled in with pride,
But wobbled a bit and took a slide.

With laughter ringing from the trees,
The snowball whispered, "Just you freeze!"
The cube stood firm, an icy bluff,
"I'm made of strength, you're just fluff!"

But as they clashed, a curious thing,
A splash of cold made their laughter ring.
They tumbled down, a frosty mess,
A sticky struggle, who'd guess the stress?

Yet in the end, as they lay low,
A friendship formed in the winter glow.
Through giggles bright, their feud did cease,
Two chilly pals found sweet release.

Sleet and Strife

A snowball flew with a playful zest,
To hit the cube, now wasn't that a jest?
With a plop and a splat, what a sight to see,
The ice had cracked, laughing joyfully!

The icy block with a chilly glare,
Retorted back with a frozen stare.
"You think you're clever, little fluff?"
"Let's see if you can hold up tough!"

They danced in circles, a slippery game,
Each tried to outdo the other's claim.
But puddles formed where laughter flowed,
And neither won as the sunlight glowed.

So here they lay, both cold and wet,
In the warmth of mirth, no reason to fret.
For what's a feud without a bit of fun?
Two frosty friends now on the run!

The Cold Confrontation

In a snowy field where the chill was clear,
Two rivals met, filled with hearty cheer.
A round of snow and a block of ice,
Which one would win in this chilly slice?

The ball rolled up with a cheeky grin,
"Come on, ice cube, let the games begin!"
With a huff and puff, the cube stood tall,
"I won't be taken down by you at all!"

A toss, a roll, a slippery play,
The crowd of snows watched in disarray.
For every throw met with a laugh,
As they grappled for their frosty path.

Then snowflakes joined, the ultimate crew,
Dancing around them as if they knew.
In the end, with spirits bright and risen,
Both claimed victory, a new decision.

Shivery Showdown

Across the field, they took their posts,
Each one a champion, or maybe just hosts.
A ball of fluff, all soft and round,
An ice cube fierce, yet rarely found.

They squared off under a sky of gray,
All the chilliness turned into play.
The round one giggled, a cheeky jest,
While the cube stayed cool, preparing its best.

With a throw and a spin, the antics began,
A battle of wit, who's the better one?
As laughter erupted, they stumbled about,
And all of the friends gathered to shout.

In a splash of snow and a great frozen cheer,
Both claimed it was fun, not who would steer.
For in every clash and each icy duel,
They found that together was really quite cool.

Winter's Tension: Snow's Bite vs. Ice's Chill

In the corner, fluffy balls, ready to throw,
Each snowflake dreams of the fun in the snow.
Ice cubes are plotting their chilly attack,
While snow whispers softly, "I've got your back."

With a squishy crunch and a slippery slide,
The battle erupts in winter's cold pride.
Puffs of pure whiteness fly through the air,
While cubes glide and clatter, with frosty flair.

Laughter erupts as the chaos unfolds,
Tiny warriors weave stories, daring and bold.
Slid into a snowbank, a comical sight,
Just watch as they tumble, a frosty delight!

In the heart of the battle, the merriment swells,
With giggles and snowflakes, and jingly bells.
Who will reign supreme in this chilly round?
It's all in good fun, the laughter resound!

Spheres of Winter: A Clash of Titans

A snowball amassed, gleaming and round,
An ice cube just grinned, looking quite proud.
The air all a-tingle, with playful intent,
Let the winter games start, with much merriment!

Rolling and tossing, a flurry of white,
Each cube counterattacks, slipping with might.
Yet snow sticks together, a fluffy brigade,
While icicles dangle, ready to invade.

The ground turns to laughter, a playground of cheer,
Snow men are crafted, with a sparkle of beer.
While cubes bounce about, making glissading trails,
Giggles erupt as each icy dodge fails.

In this arena where nothing's so serious,
Chilly antics unfold with moments quite glorious.
For in the end, as the laughter subsides,
Winter's the victor, as joy abides!

Icicle Incursion: Parade of Frost

Here come the snowflakes, a parade on the run,
Puffy and jolly, they dance in the sun.
Ice cubes in formation, slick and so brave,
They're ready to rumble, in the vast winter grave.

With a whoosh and a zoom, the snowballs take flight,
While the cubes roll in patterns, oh, what a sight!
Giggles erupt as the flurries collide,
Each icy encounter bringing laughter worldwide.

In a swirl of chaos, the games take their turn,
With pointed attacks that make everyone yearn.
The frosty brigade spins in frolicking glee,
Bringing warmth to the hearts, with each funny spree.

Glorious moments of snow versus ice,
In this musical battle, nothing's too nice.
And as the sun sets on this whimsical plight,
They unite in the laughter, as day turns to night!

Powdered Fury in a Frozen Realm

Stomp, stomp through the snow, on a quest for some fun,
Who will win this tussle? The snow or the gun?
With powdered adventures in a frosty terrain,
Both sides throw blows in a whimsical game!

The snowballs burst forth like giggles at play,
While ice cubes skitter, slipping away.
Laughter like jingles fills up the skies,
As winter's own chaos invites joyful sighs.

Splotches of white launch from hands full of glee,
In a dance of pure delight, they tumble, carefree.
The icy revenge as they bounce with a flair,
Only fuels the antics of this frosty affair.

A skirmish of legends, both funny and bright,
In a swirl of soft snowflakes, oh, what a sight!
With friendships ignited amid laughter and cheer,
This wintertime battle brings all the warmth near!

Surfacing Rivalries in the Snow

Two creatures in the glistening white,
One rolls and one darts with icy might.
Snowballs fly with laughter and cheer,
While cubes plot laughter far and near.

Chillin' on corners, plotting in style,
Snowman grins wide, it's been a while.
Icy cube hurls a frozen little ball,
But miss! Oh dear! Down goes the wall!

A dance of joy in the crisp chilly air,
Snowflakes tumble like they just don't care.
With cheeky laughs and snow-covered glee,
Who knew winter could be so free?

Thus the fluffy laughter continues to play,
In a winter wonderland, they frolic all day.
With a wink and a swirl, the fun carries on,
As rivalries melt with the coming dawn.

Icebound Embers: Duel of Cold Creatures

In a realm where chill meets a cheeky grin,
Flurries fly fast, let the games begin!
A cube hides slyly behind the old tree,
While snowballs are rolling, full of glee.

With playful jabs, the battle ignites,
One slips in snow, while the other just bites.
A toss, a dive, oh what a grand scene,
Where ice and snow make a frosty cuisine!

Giggles erupt from both sides of the fray,
As snow splats down in a lively ballet.
With each chilly throw, the laughter erupts,
An icy confrontation, oh how it disrupts!

In the end, they sit, all bundled and frozen,
With frozen hearts warmed, feelings now chosen.
Battles forgotten, giggles ensue,
For nothing's quite like a cold friend so true!

A Tempest in a Snow Globe

In a globe where worlds collide and twirl,
Snowballs whistle as the frosty winds whirl.
A pop and a crash, a cube takes aim,
But snowflakes giggle; it's all just a game.

With snowmen cheering, the action unfolds,
Each icy clash is a story retold.
Round and round in this snowy delight,
Where laughter spills through the thick winter night.

Cubes of ice roll with cheeky finesse,
Chasing snowballs in this chilly mess.
What chaos it brings, oh, what a sight,
In this dome of fun, filled with pure light!

As the storm settles in a silvery shroud,
With fun and camaraderie, echoing loud.
A united front, come spark if you dare,
In this globe of frost, there's plenty to share!

The Winter's Thaw: A Conflict Renewed

As spring peeks shyly with warmth on its breath,
The frozen squabbles are challenged by depth.
But wait! Here's a snowball with mischief so bright,
A cube's just around, plotting a laugh-filled bite.

Splat! The snowball as it flies through the air,
Toward the ice cube, with no time for despair.
A laugh erupts like a crack in the ice,
While the cube grumbles back, "Now that's not so nice!"

Across fields of white, they scamper and glide,
These chilly foes making memories to bide.
With every throw, the joy moves more clear,
As friendships form, chased by winter's dear cheer.

So let's toast with snow cones and battles anew,
With laughter that dances in skies shining blue.
In this thawing delight of frosty designer,
No rivalry can last when the fun is a sign-er!

Shivers of Contest: Ice and Snow Collide

In a field of white, they stand tall,
A round ball of fluff, and a cube so small.
Laughter erupts as they take their aim,
Who will win in this silly game?

Cold clouds gather, the tension does rise,
Both combatants ready with gleeful eyes.
With a squish and a thunk, they let it fly,
Hilarity reigns, as they both aim high!

The snowball sails with a giggle and twirl,
While the ice cube slides with a slippery whirl.
Onlookers chuckle at the chilly delight,
As they chase each other, what a funny sight!

When the sun peeks out, and they both slip,
Into a puddle, with a sploosh and a drip.
Laughter rings out, as they melt away,
The battle of frosty fun ends in a play!

Frigid Fray: The War of Winter's Shapes

In snow-capped laughter, they both engage,
A fluffy round fighter, and a block on a stage.
With fierce determination, they roll and they glide,
In this wintery battle, they both take pride.

Snowflakes surround, making it all bright,
As ice skates away, trying to take flight.
Ping! The first hit, a snowball's delight,
A crash and a splat, oh, what a sight!

Dodging and weaving, they dance in the snow,
A freeze and a slip, who would've known?
With giggles and squeals, they leap through the air,
In the midst of this winter, nothing can compare!

As evening approaches, the fun starts to fade,
But memories linger of the frosty parade.
In the heart of the blizzard, they simply proclaim,
Let's do this again; let's savor the game!

Bullet vs. Slab: A Chilling Encounter

A bullet made of snow with a laugh and a dash,
A slab of ice ready to make quite a splash.
With giggles and glee, the frosty fun starts,
In this whimsical clash of wintery arts.

As the snowball launches with speed and a cheer,
The ice cube braces, fully aware of the fear.
With a thud and a bang, the clash rings out clear,
Justice will freeze in this frigid frontier!

Sliding and tumbling, the two chase around,
With squeals of delight, in the laughter they're bound.
They roll and they tumble, all slippery and spry,
A duel turned to dancing, neither will die!

But as twilight descends, they start to unite,
With a truce made of giggles, their hearts feel so light.
Though in combat they played, it's fun that they seek,
In this frosty arena, friendships they peek!

Whiteout War: Nature's Competition

In the frostbitten air, they gather their might,
A fluffy white ball and a cube dressed in white.
Laughter erupts as they come face to face,
In this wacky contest of chill and of grace.

Snowflakes flutter down in a sparkling dance,
While icy intentions are stirred by chance.
With a whoosh and a squish, the laughter takes flight,
As snow meets the ice in the crisp winter night!

Chilly chuckles echo from all around,
As the ball bounces brightly, thundering sound.
Blocks of ice shatter in the frenzy of fun,
In this merry commotion, laughter's just begun!

But as moonlight glimmers, the frosty face grins,
With warmed hearts they gather, embracing their wins.
For the joy of the snow, and the ice that can freeze,
In this game, it's together, just play as you please!

Crystal Clash: A Winter's Duel

Two frosty warriors take their stand,
With silly grins, they form their brand.
One packs soft balls, fluffy and round,
The other throws cubes without a sound.

Laughter echoes across the field,
As icy shields begin to yield.
Snow flies high and sticks like glue,
Who'll slip on the glimmering avenue?

Chilly giggles fill the scene,
Masked in frost, they play obscene.
Piles of snowballs scatter wide,
While cubes slip, learning to glide.

Up in the air, a snowball throws,
A cube just tumbles, oh the woes!
Friends or foes, who can tell?
In this battle, all's jolly swell!

Snowbound Showdown

In the park where snowflakes spin,
Two friends prepare to dive right in.
Soft spheres of snow and icy bricks,
With each throw comes cold comedy tricks.

Laughter reigns as they tumble down,
Clumsy forms cover the town.
With each impact, giggles arise,
The chilly air filled with funny cries.

A snowball whizzes through the air,
Missing the target, oh what a scare!
While ice cubes chime like little bells,
Making music as laughter swells.

In this playful winter show,
Snow and ice steal the show!
With each round, the fun ascends,
A merry duel where joy never ends!

The Icy Encounter of Chill and Thrill

Beneath the trees, snow blankets white,
Two pals engage in playful spite.
One's armed with powder, fluffy and bright,
The other, sharp cubes, a frigid bite.

They hurl their weapons, giggling loud,
As snow drifts join the cheering crowd.
Slips and slides are the order of day,
Each one hoping for a frosty display.

In the midst of frosty chase,
They toss and roll with grinning face.
Laughter sparkles on winter's breath,
As cubes and snowballs dance with death.

The snowy ground, a canvas to paint,
Of playful joy, never quaint.
In this chilly game of fun and cheers,
They forget the world, lose all fears.

Frosted Combat: Pellets vs. Cubes

In a field of ice where spirits soar,
Two foes prepare for snowball war.
One's artillery is fluffy and fine,
While the other constructs cubes that shine.

They charge and clash with all their might,
Creating chaos, oh what a sight!
Laughter bursts with every throw,
As snowflakes dance in a swirling flow.

The cubes launch fast but slip and slide,
While soft snowballs dance with pride.
In this joyful bout of icy cheer,
Who'll reign supreme, my dear?

As night falls, they crown the fun,
Grinning wide, their battle won.
For in this frosty, giggly fight,
Friendship sparkles, pure delight!

Permafrost Showdown: Chaos Under White

In a world of snow so bright,
A snowball rolled with all its might.
An ice cube glared in the sun,
Ready to freeze the fun begun.

They danced and dashed in crisp, clear air,
A frosty battle, unaware.
With giggles echoing, they took a stand,
A frozen duel, oh, what a plan!

The snowball flew and missed the mark,
While the ice cube glinted in the dark.
"Slide on over!" the snowball cried,
"Let's see who wins this chilly ride!"

But the ice cube slipped, oh what a blunder,
The snowball laughed, as thunder flundered.
As snowflakes snowed all over the scene,
That wacky war turned quite obscene!

The Ice Age Chronicles: Conflict in Cold

Two foes emerged from winter's hold,
A snowball big, an ice cube bold.
They plotted schemes, so sweet and sly,
In laughter's grip, they both did fly.

The snowball rolled with zest and cheer,
While the ice cube gleamed, crystal clear.
"Let's race!" the snowball called with glee,
"Catch me if you can, oh icy tea!"

Through flurries thick, they went amiss,
A tumble here, a frozen kiss.
Slippery paths and giggles galore,
"Who knew a fight could be such a chore?"

At the end of it, with a big surprise,
They shared a laugh under winter skies.
With frosty fists, the burden melted,
As joy and warmth in their hearts settled!

Winter's Clash

In the chill of a winter morn,
A snowball and ice cube got sworn.
With gleeful laughter in the air,
They hatched a plot to cause some scare.

The snowball bounced with a splashy pounce,
While the ice cube grinned, not one to flounce.
"Take that!" yelled snow, flying fast and bright,
As the ice cube glimmered, ready for a fight!

Around the yard, they tumbled and pranced,
In a clumsy little battle, they fiercely danced.
One would roll and the other would slide,
With giggles pouring like an icy tide.

What a ruckus, a hilarious sight,
Who knew cold could be sheer delight?
They ended up as buddies too,
In a frosty hug, not a foe in view!

Chill and Thrill

A snowball plopped with a playful cheer,
An ice cube slipped, 'Oh dear, oh dear!'
Frolicking amid the snowy plains,
They twirled and whirled, ignoring their pains.

"Let's see who can freeze the other one first!"
Proclaimed the cube, with a frosty burst.
The snowball giggled, "That's quite a feat,
But can you handle my chilly retreat?"

Daring dashes turned into laughs,
While icy blasts balanced on their paths.
Snowball flew, and oh, what a mess,
With ice cube's chill, a giggly excess!

As the sunset painted skies so bright,
They wrapped up their playful fight.
United in fun, with smiles so wide,
Who knew winter's chill could bring such pride?

Glittering Gauntlet

In the park where laughter roams,
Snowballs fly like tiny gnomes.
Ice cubes stare with frosty might,
Claiming victory in the night.

Laughter echoes, a comical sight,
The snowball's grin, oh so bright.
Ice cubes shiver, plotting their chance,
To join the joyful, snowy dance.

With each toss, they giggle and roll,
A winter war that warms the soul.
The ground is white, the sky a thrill,
Only the brave dare to take their fill.

As snowflakes fall, a truce is near,
Winks and nudges, no room for fear.
They bundle up for cocoa's cheer,
For in this game, friends are always near.

Polar Parley

Two frosty foes of winter's best,
Engage in frolic, not in jest.
With snowballs launched and ice cubes coy,
They battle hard, but share the joy.

A flurry of laughter fills the air,
As icy shards fly everywhere.
The snow's like glitter, shining bright,
In this zany, chilly fight.

A snowball lands with a splat and squish,
Oh, how they dream of a snowy wish!
Ice cubes melt in the warm embrace,
The friendly punchline of the chase.

"Let's make a truce," the snowball said,
"After the next fun hit to the head!"
So they raised their mugs of cocoa warm,
Cheers to laughter, in this winter charm!

Frosty Foes

Ice cubes shiver, snowballs gleam,
Each has a point, a bold little beam.
With laughter erupting, they take their fling,
In this chilly game, the joy does sing.

Bouncing off cheeks, they duel and clash,
Snowball giggles, you hear the crash.
Ice cubes plotting, with a cheeky grin,
Who will be the frosty kingpin?

A dash here, a twirl there, watch them flee,
Each chase is a splash of glee!
A world of white, where fun abounds,
Echoes of laughter are all around.

So join the fray, don't miss the fun,
With every toss, a new battle sprung.
Together united, foes turned to friends,
In this winter tale, the laughter never ends.

The Icy Interlude

A snowball's surprise, it takes flight,
While ice cubes conspire in frosty delight.
They giggle and toss, like kids at play,
Turning the chill into a riotous fray.

The snowball rolls with a fluffy cheer,
While ice cubes wobble, awfully near.
They hurl and tumble, landing in heaps,
When giggles emerge, their frosty hearts leap.

With each chilly launch, the laughter grows,
In a snowy arena where glee overflows.
The wind whispers secrets, the trees sway around,
In this wintery realm, joy knows no bounds.

A final showdown with a wink and a cheer,
They clasp each other, no hint of fear.
For in this skirmish of laughter and play,
They found their friendship, in a snowy ballet.

Whirlwind of White

In a flurry they came, all dressed in white,
Laughter erupted, oh what a sight!
Snowballs whizzed by, like bullets in flight,
While ice cubes plotted in shadows of night.

The air filled with giggles, a chilly delight,
Each throw felt like candy, a sugary bite.
A snowball brigade, ready to ignite,
While ice cubes just laughed, feeling quite spright.

Towering mounds formed, as laughter amassed,
With slippery slides, they flew by so fast!
Their dance was hilarious, which made time last,
In the war of the winter—oh, what a blast!

As snow fell like glitter, they played till the end,
For no one could tell where the chaos would blend.
A mountain of giggles, where laughter would mend,
In this whirlwind of fun, each foe became friend.

Snowflake Showdown

Gather 'round, folks, for a flake-filled fight,
With flurries of fun, we'll dance through the night.
Snowballs in hand, we'll launch with delight,
While ice cubes keep sliding, trying to bite.

The bold and the brave went toe-to-toe,
Chaining giggles in frosty tableau.
Ice cubes would chime, "Just try us, you know!"
Yet each frosty throw made their confidence low.

With a plop and a splash, the snowballs took flight,
While ice cubes just tumbled, they lost the height.
"Be cool!" one snowball shouted with might,
As laughter lit up the chilly moonlight.

In friendly mayhem, both sides took their turn,
With each icy blast, there was plenty to learn.
Neither side conquers, it's all part of the churn,
In this silly showdown, let the laughter burn!

The Chilling Challenge

Come one, come all, to the chilling affair,
Where snowballs unite with a frosty flair.
A challenge begins in the brisk winter air,
With each cheeky throw, we've lost all despair.

Ice cubes were sneaky, they hid in the snow,
With plans to surprise—"Here we go, here we go!"
But snowballs erupted, like bubbles in dough,
With laughter and joy making hearts all aglow.

Frolicking fun in this freezing contest,
Every throw felt like a playful jest.
An icy ambush, nobody would rest,
Till all were defeat—oh what a quest!

In childish delight, they battled with cheer,
Through layers of laughter, no sign of fear.
With smiles so wide and intentions so clear,
The challenge was won, but the joy lingered near.

Frost and Fury

From the shadows arose, the icicles gleamed,
Snowball warriors plotting, or so it seemed.
Together they gathered, both silly and steamed,
In a frosty adventure, where laughter beamed.

As snowballs were formed, they grinned ear to ear,
While ice cubes just glimmered, shivering in fear.
"Let us show them, we're the champions here!"
The snowballs replied, echoing loud and clear.

With a throw and a splash, they leaped into fray,
Ice cubes retaliated, but who would win today?
In this battle of banter, no one led astray,
With each chuckle shared, they found their own way.

So here's to the chaos, the fun ever near,
With frosty ambition fueled by good cheer.
From snowflakes to ice, let's raise up a beer,
To laughter and joy, let the good times endear!

Milton Keynes UK
Ingram Content Group UK Ltd.
UKHW020817141124
451205UK00012B/633

9 789916 942758